ULTIMATE GUIDE TO CALIFORNIA'S PRELIMINARY NOTICE

By Scott G. Wolfe, Jr.

Published by Zlien

Lien Smart. Get Paid.

© 2012

Ultimate Guide To California's Preliminary Notice

Library of Congress

ISBN 978-1-300-30683-2

Publisher: Lulu Enterprises, Inc.

Printed in the United States of America

By Scott G. Wolfe, Jr.   Published by Zlien

ABOUT SCOTT G. WOLFE, Jr.

Scott calls himself the "mechanics lien guru" on his short twitter profile (@scottwolfejr). As a seasoned construction attorney, Scott has helped contractors and suppliers across the country litigate mechanics lien and bond claim actions. Through his practice he saw a need for a smart lien compliance solution, and thus Zlien was born.

Scott currently serves as Zlien's CEO, and is the founding author of the Lien Blog. As CEO, he has guided the company through a round of fundraising and acquired $450,000 of seed capital. He has also led the company through year-over-year growth, most recently by growing Zlien's revenue over 700% in the 2011 calendar year.

Scott lives in New Orleans with his wife and daughter, but travels frequently and works in Seattle, WA during the summer months.

Scott is a licensed construction attorney in six states (CA, AZ, WA, OR, GA, LA), and the founding partner of Wolfe Law Group, a multi-state construction law firm. His law practice is now very limited, as he serves full time as Zlien's CEO.

ABOUT ZLIEN

Zlien (http://www.zlien.com) is a venture-backed mechanics lien, preliminary notice, and bond claim compliance service.

Through its proprietary LienPilot web application, Zlien helps contractors and suppliers manage its lien and notice deadlines nationwide. Through its legal document preparation services, Zlien can have documents sent and filed across the country with just the click of a button.

Zlien also publishes the web's most comprehensive mechanics lien and bond claim resources free of charge. Contractors and suppliers can use these resources to reference the lien and bond claim remedies available to them on private, state, or federal construction projects.

By Scott G. Wolfe, Jr.   Published by Zlien

CONTENTS

By Scott G. Wolfe, Jr.   Published by Zlien

CHAPTER 2

California's Preliminary Notice Requirement.................................**17**

CHAPTER 3

Details About California's Preliminary Notice Requirements.......**23**

By Scott G. Wolfe, Jr.   Published by Zlien

8

California Preliminary Notice For Private Projects Form & Instructions 53

California Preliminary Notice For State, County, Municipal Projects Form & Instructions 57

By Scott G. Wolfe, Jr.   Published by Zlien

FAST FACTS

PRIVATE PROJECTS	STATE PROJECTS
Those who do not contract with the owner must send preliminary notice to the: • Direct Contractor • Property Owner • Construction Lender (if any) Those who contract with the owner must send preliminary notice to the: • Construction Lender (if any)	Those who do not contract with the public entity commissioning work must send preliminary notice to: • Direct Contractor • Public Entity • Surety

RULES THAT APPLY TO BOTH STATE AND PRIVATE PROJECTS
• Must send within 20 days of first furnishing labor, materials, or services to the project • Notice must be sent by certified mail • Must maintain a copy of the notice sent, a declaration of delivery (confirming who the notice was sent to), how it was sent, and the method of sending • Late notices are effective for materials, labor, or services furnished within 20 days of the notice's delivery, and beyond • A Preliminary notice form must meet statutory requirements, include specific language in boldface type, and include an "estimate" of the total value of your services

The *Ultimate Guide to California's Preliminary Notice* is up-to-date with California's current lien law, which took effect July 1, 2012.

By Scott G. Wolfe, Jr.   Published by Zlien

CHAPTER 1

What Is Preliminary Notice?

WHAT IS PRELIMINARY NOTICE?

Some states require preliminary notices while others do not. In the states where preliminary notice is required, a party providing labor and/or materials must deliver a notice to certain other parties before or immediately after they begin performing work or providing materials. If the notice is required and not sent, you may lose the right to later file a lien if you are not paid.

WHAT TYPES OF NOTICES ARE THERE? ARE THEY MANDATORY?

While the term "notice" gets used a great deal in construction circles, many contractors do not understand what is meant by "notice." Is it a "notice of intent to lien?" Is it a pre-work "preliminary notice?" The difference between notice types is discussed in following sections.

Furthermore, notices are not required in every state. For states that do require notices, the types of notices can be vastly different. Determining requirements can be difficult, but Zlien's **LienPilot** can calculate your notice requirements based on your job information.

HOW ARE PRELIMINARY NOTICES SENT?

This is a very important question. If your state requires certain notices and you send them incorrectly, it may be just as bad as not sending notices at all. Accordingly, sending the notice as required by statute is very, very important. You must check the delivery requirements as they vary substantially by state.

By Scott G. Wolfe, Jr.   Published by Zlien

It is safe to say that most states require preliminary notices to be sent by certified mail, or certified mail with return receipt requested. There are some instances, however, when notices must be sent by registered mail only, by mail with restricted delivery, hand delivered by courier, and/or actually filed with the county recorder.

It is just as important to prove that you delivered the notice, as it is to deliver the notice correctly. California has some fairly strict requirements in this regard, which can give you an idea of what you will confront in proving preliminary notice delivery elsewhere. In California, parties serving preliminary notices by mail must maintain an affidavit of delivery and a copy of the return receipt card (or other U.S. postage delivery record). A very minor deviation from the statute's requirement can be fatal to your lien claim.

A NATIONWIDE BIG PICTURE LOOK AT PRELIMINARY NOTICES

This section examines the preliminary notice document without focusing on any particular state's requirements, and may help you understand how these things generally work. With a better general appreciation for the preliminary notice, you can then turn to the state's particular requirements and have a better chance at complying with these requirements.

WHY PRELIMINARY NOTICES ARE IMPORTANT TO CONTRACTORS & SUPPLIERS

Mechanic's liens are a very effective legal tool for contractors, subcontractors, equipment lenders and suppliers. If you're having trouble getting paid in the construction industry, or if your credit policy isn't quite producing the paying customers you've always dreamed about, you can significantly decrease your ratio of bad debts and your bottom line by paying attention to your lien rights.

Ever not get paid because the party who hired you couldn't get paid? Ever not get paid because the party who hired you filed bankruptcy? A mechanic's lien can help you avoid these situations, allowing you to leapfrog the party who hired you, and can bring a lawsuit or claim directly against the property owner.

By Scott G. Wolfe, Jr.   Published by Zlien

DO THESE RULES APPLY TO ANY PARTICULAR STATE?

No. This guide is written to provide you with a general overview of preliminary notice requirements on all types of construction projects (federal, state and private) in every state.

The positive here is that if you are supplying materials or services to multiple states, this general overview will be helpful. The negative is that you still have to consult with each state's laws for specific requirements, as every state's notice requirements are different.

SO WHAT IS A PRELIMINARY NOTICE ANYWAY?

As I mentioned, the right to file a mechanic's lien is a significant and powerful legal remedy. In its own way, every state balances the interest of the supplier or laborer (in getting paid for work) with the interest of the property owner (in not being required to pay twice for construction). A large number of states find a balance of these interests with their preliminary notice requirements.

To preserve your right to file a lien, you must notify certain parties that you are performing work or furnishing materials. The notification must occur immediately after you start work. If you deliver the notice, you are allowed to later file a lien. If you don't, you have no lien rights at all.

ARE PRELIMINARY NOTICES REQUIRED IN EVERY STATE?

No, they are not required in every state. States that require notice include: Alaska, Arizona, Arkansas, California, Florida, Kentucky, Maryland, Massachusetts, Michigan, Minnesota, Montana, Nevada, New Hampshire, New Mexico, Ohio, Oklahoma, Oregon, South Carolina, South Dakota, Tennessee, Texas, Utah, Washington, Wisconsin, and Wyoming.

Non-notice states include: Alabama, Colorado, Connecticut, Delaware, Georgia (unless owner files Notice of Commencement), Hawaii, Idaho, Illinois (Except on Owner Occupied Residential Construction), Indiana (Except on Owner Occupied Residential Construction), Iowa (Except on Owner Occupied Residential Construction), Kansas, Louisiana (except

13

for equipment lessons), Maine, Mississippi, Missouri, Nebraska, New Jersey, New York, North Carolina (unless Notice of Contract filed by prime contractor), North Dakota, Pennsylvania, Rhode Island, Vermont, Virginia (Except on residential construction when Mechanic Lien Agent identified), West Virginia, and Washington D.C.

Here is a color-coded U.S. map of preliminary notice requirements.

HOW DO WE FILE THESE PRELIMINARY NOTICES?

Filing preliminary notices can be tricky because each state is different in its requirements for how the notice must be sent, who must receive it, when it must be sent, and what the form must say.

If you are only doing business in one state, and usually performing within the same tier, you may be able to get the form for your situation and have someone at your office learn the process and send notices out. However, why would you want to waste the time of your employees?

If you are in multiple states or doing work on a lot of projects, you're likely going to need help. Getting the help is worth it. Help will free your staff to do things they should be doing (i.e. making you money), and leaves the technical and time-consuming notice work to someone who does it day-in and day-out.

Check out a company like Zlien (http://www.zlien.com), who files preliminary notices all across the country. Zlien puts together and delivers a notice for you after you send information about any new construction projects or supply contracts.

Using Zlien is a lot more convenient that rummaging through Internet articles about each state's notice requirements, using the notice company's software to breakdown the lien laws, and figuring out what gets sent, when, and how.

IS THERE ONE NOTICE FORM WE CAN USE FOR EVERY STATE?

While every state's forms contain similar information, they are not the same. Many states require that very specific language is included in the notice. Sometimes, states require

By Scott G. Wolfe, Jr.   Published by Zlien

the notice to be in a certain font size, in all caps, or bolded, which makes it nearly impossible to have one form for every state and every situation.

ALL NOTICES ARE NOT CREATED EQUAL: PRELIMINARY NOTICE VS. NOTICE OF INTENT TO LIEN

In the world of construction liens, the word "Notice" gets frequent use. The technical nature of each state's notice requirements is often misunderstood. In general, there are two types of "notices" required by lien statutes: (1) Preliminary Notice and (2) Notice of Intent to Lien.

PRELIMINARY NOTICE VS. NOTICE OF INTENT TO LIEN

A "Preliminary Notice" must usually be provided to the notified party before work begins on a construction project, or within a certain time frame from when materials are first furnished.

A "Notice of Intent to Lien," on the other hand, must usually be provided to the notified party before filing a lien. This can range from seven to fifteen days prior.

As you can see from these simple definitions, the requirements are extremely different. It's safe to assume that if your project and state require notice, the failure to send it will result in forfeiture of your company's lien rights.

WHEN IS NOTICE REQUIRED?

Every state's requirements are different – and unfortunately, quite technical. Not only does the technical nature of lien statutes make them difficult to understand and interpret, but they also result in sometimes-absurd consequences.

Here are some general notice trends:

❖ **Frequent Rule #1:** Almost every state has notice requirements when work is

15

By Scott G. Wolfe, Jr.   Published by Zlien

being performed on an "owner-occupied" residence. In theory, this is to protect homeowners from getting burned and having to pay contractors twice. Some states (like Pennsylvania) even prohibit liens against single-family homeowner residences.

❖ **Frequent Rule #2:** The further down the chain you are, the more likely notice is required. Across the nation, there are more notice requirements for subcontractors than prime contractors, and more notice requirements for sub-subcontractors and suppliers than first tier subcontractors.

Zlien is a publisher of some of the web's best free resources for construction lien laws in the United States. Aside from this resource, check out MechanicLein.com where you can get charts explaining lien deadlines, notice deadlines, and download free forms. The site allows you to check your state's lien laws if you're working on everything from an "owner-occupied" residence to contracting with a subcontractor.

By Scott G. Wolfe, Jr.   Published by Zlien

CHAPTER 2

California's Preliminary Notice Requirement

BROAD OVERVIEW OF PRELIMINARY NOTICE REQUIREMENT

In California, if you provide materials or labor to a construction project, you are generally allowed to lien that project in the event of non-payment. In some circumstances, however, California law requires that a claimant provide notice to certain parties to preserve its rights to lien.

This notice is commonly referred to as "Preliminary 20-day Notice," although a law modification that went into effect on July 1, 2012 changed the terminology and it is now called simply a "Preliminary Notice". Contrary to popular belief, the notice must be sent to the required parties as soon as or before work begins, and not simply before a lien is filed.

WHAT IS PRELIMINARY 20-DAY NOTICE?

California Civil Code § 8200 provides that notice "means a written notice from a claimant that is given prior to the recording of a mechanic's lien…"

The California preliminary notice requirements are similar to the requirements of other states, and they serve to notify the property owner that the property may be liened in the event of non-payment.

A construction lien carries severe consequences to the property owner. If a property owner pays the general contractor who fails to pay its subs, the owner may be obligated to pay twice on the project through a construction lien. Most states require preliminary notice to ensure that the owner is notified of who is and who is not working on their property.

THE FORM OF CALIFORNIA'S PRELIMINARY NOTICE

California statute requires that preliminary notices contain specific information. California Civil Code § 8102 provides that the notice must contain the following:

- Name and address of the owner or reputed owner

- Name and address of the director contractor

- Name and address of the construction lender, if any

- Description of the site sufficient for identification, including the site street address, if any

- Name, address, and relationship to the parties of the person giving notice

- General statement of the work provided

- The name of the person to or for whom the work is provided

Further requirements are enumerated in a separate section of the California statutes, Civ. Code § 8202, which provides that in addition to complying with §8102⊠s requirements, a preliminary notice must also include:

- A general description of the work to be provided

- An estimate of the total price of the work to be provided

- The following, exact statement in **boldface** type:

NOTICE TO PROPERTY OWNER EVEN THOUGH YOU HAVE PAID YOUR CONTRACTOR IN FULL, if the person or firm that has given you this notice is not paid in full for labor, service, equipment, or material provided or to be provided to your construction project, a lien may be placed on your property. Foreclosure of the lien may lead to loss of all or part of your property. You may wish to protect yourself against this by (1) requiring your contractor to provide a signed release by the person or firm that has given you this notice before making

By Scott G. Wolfe, Jr.   Published by Zlien

payment to your contractor, or (2) any other method that is appropriate under the circumstances. This notice is required by law to be served by the undersigned as a statement of your legal rights. This notice is not intended to reflect upon the financial condition of the contractor or the person employed by you on the construction project. If you record a notice of cessation or completion of your construction project, you must within 10 days after recording, send a copy of the notice of completion to your contractor and the person or firm that has given you this notice.

The notice must be sent by registered or certified mail. Failure to send the notice will extend the deadline to record a claim of lien. However, you are not required to send the notice if you are a residential homeowner of a dwelling containing four or fewer units.

Since these requirements are set forth by statute, and lien statutes are strictly construed, it is important that your preliminary notice meet these requirements. A free template of a California Preliminary Notice form for both state and private projects can be found here and here, respectively.

WHO MUST PROVIDE NOTICE

As discussed above, not everyone is required to provide this Preliminary Notice. There are many circumstances when a contractor or supplier can lien a project when they have not sent preliminary notice. However, this occurs in the minority of cases, and recent case law along with the July 1st 2012 law change in California has made it more rare. The key problem, therefore, is identifying who must provide Preliminary Notice.

The new general rule for California is that Preliminary Notice is required by anyone who is not a laborer. A laborer is defined as someone who performs purely labor work on a project, and does not provide materials.

Additionally, those in direct contract with the owner have reduced preliminary notice requirements. In many cases, they do not need to send preliminary notice. In the case of those parties in direct contract with the property owner, preliminary notice need only be sent to the construction lender, if there is one.

By Scott G. Wolfe, Jr.   Published by Zlien

Interestingly, California courts have very liberally construed the phrase "direct contract with the owner" to include other parties aside from those who actually signed the contract with the owner. Any contractor or material man is presumed to be under "direct contract" with the owner so long as the owner has actual knowledge that construction work is being performed on his property. [*Kim v. JF Enterprises* (App 2. Dist. 1996) 50 Cal. Rptr. 2d 141, 42 Cal. App. 4th 849] Be cautious about this precedent, however, as it is from before the July 1st amendments.

WHERE TO SEND A CALIFORNIA PRELIMINARY NOTICE

Assuming you are required to send Preliminary Notice, the California statutes stipulate exactly who is required to receive that notice to properly preserve a contractor or supplier's lien rights.

The Preliminary Notice should be sent to all of the following:

- The Owner (or reputed owner)

- The Original Contractor (or reputed original contractor)

- The construction lender, if any

Of course, as above-mentioned, those who contract directly with the owner need only send notice to the construction lender.

WHEN TO SEND A CALIFORNIA PRELIMINARY NOTICE

Perhaps the most important question about preliminary notice in California concerns when the statutes require that a contractor or supplier deliver notice.

In California, notice must be given not later than 20 days after the claimant has first furnished labor, services, equipment or materials to the jobsite. After the expiration of these 20 days, the claimant may still send notice, but it will only be effective as to the labor, services, and materials supplied or provided within 20 days prior to the service of the notice (and thereafter).

Therefore, if you are required to provide preliminary notice under California statutes, it is imperative that you deliver the notice as soon as is practical. Waiting until 20 days after you begin work will jeopardize your rights to lien for unpaid work.

HOW TO SEND A CALIFORNIA PRELIMINARY NOTICE

California statutes specifically provide a method for sending notice to the receiving parties.

The notice can be sent by delivering the document personally, by leaving it at the residence or place of business of the party with some person in charge, or by registered or certified first-class mail. If the owner is out of state and these methods do not work, you can send the owner's notice via certified or registered mail to the construction lender or original contractor.

It is important to keep good records of delivery, as the statutes also provide a specific method to prove the preliminary notice was delivered. In fact, the statute requires that you keep a "Proof of Notice Declaration" that states the type of notice given, the date, the place and manner of giving notice, facts showing the notice was given as required by the statute, the name and address of the person to which notice was given, and some documentation showing the tracking and delivery of the same if the notice was given my mail. See California Civil Code § 8118.

WHY YOU SHOULD USE ZLIEN TO SEND YOUR CALIFORNIA PRELIMINARY NOTICES

As you can see, properly sending a California preliminary notice requires a lot of compliance. The detailed and ever-changing nature of the law make it best to rely on Zlien and its proprietary preliminary notice and mechanics lien compliance system to ensure your preliminary notices are sent right, all of the time.

Every time Zlien sends a California preliminary notice, it performs the following:

- Researches the property owner and lender to confirm identity

- Prepares the form and delivers it to the required parties

21

- Pays for all postage

- Tracks mailings to ensure delivery

- Keeps an Affidavit and Declaration of Delivery

Zlien is a licensed, bonded and insured legal document preparation company in the State of California (LDA-352).

By Scott G. Wolfe, Jr.   Published by Zlien

CHAPTER 3

Details About California's Preliminary Notice Requirements

3 IMPORTANT DETAILS ABOUT CALIFORNIA'S PRELIMINARY NOTICE REQUIREMENT

California's preliminary notice requirement is fairly straightforward, but is saturated with detail. This Legal Guide discusses three important nuances of the California mechanics lien laws that may affect the validity of your California preliminary notice.

NOTICES CAN NEVER BE SENT TOO EARLY...AND LATE NOTICES MAY BE OKAY

You may know that the California preliminary notice must be sent within "20 days of first furnishing labor and materials" on the construction project. But, this begs two questions: What happens if the notice is sent early, and what happens if the notice is sent late? Unlike some states (like Ohio), you can never send a preliminary notice too early in California. You can send your preliminary notice weeks or months before the scheduled first delivery, including when you first sign your contract, and the preliminary notice will be effective.

It is possible to send a late preliminary notice in California as well, but the rules are not as liberal. While notices can be sent late in California, they are only effective for labor or materials furnished AFTER the late notice. So, since the notice is a 20-day notice, you can count back 20 days from the notice's actual delivery, and have protection of lien rights from that point forward.

23

By Scott G. Wolfe, Jr.   Published by Zlien

KEEP GOOD PROOF THAT YOU DELIVERED YOUR PRELIMINARY NOTICE

You can send preliminary notices indefinitely, but if you can't prove that you sent the preliminary notice you will be subject to penalties. There are no formal measurements of proof within the law unlike, for instance, in Arizona where the property owner and general contractor must return a slip indicating receipt of the preliminary notice. It is entirely your responsibility to keep track of your California preliminary notices and keep good detailed records of delivery. A good practice is to (i) Keep the proof of mailing and delivery from the USPS, and (ii) Draft an affidavit of mailing each time you mail out a notice.

NO NEED TO SEND ADDITIONAL PRELIMINARY NOTICES AFTER CHANGE ORDERS OR OTHER CONTRACT AMENDMENTS

California preliminary notices require you to estimate the total contract amount and indicate that right within the notice. What happens if a change order or contract amendment increases or decreases the work? Thankfully for those working in California, an additional preliminary notice is not required. So long as the change is a change order or amendment to the original contract and not an entirely new contract, California does not require a follow up preliminary notice.

BEST PRACTICES FOR SENDING CALIFORNIA'S PRELIMINARY NOTICE UNDER THE NEW LAW

New mechanics lien laws took effect in California July 1st, 2012. The new laws impact preliminary notices sent on both public and private projects in California. This post examines three best practices to employ when sending a preliminary notice document in the state.

REQUEST THE LENDER AND OWNER

One of the most significant changes for subcontractors and suppliers who frequently

By Scott G. Wolfe, Jr.   Published by Zlien

send preliminary notices is that California law now creates an affirmative duty for direct contractors to "make available" the name and address of the property owner and the lender.

This used to be a terrible headache for those required to deliver these preliminary notices. They were required to notify the owner and lender, but had no efficient means of finding the identity of these parties. Now, however, the direct contractor must provide this information.

In crafting a best practice for California preliminary notices you should keep this obligation in mind, and take advantage of it on the preliminary notice. When sending a preliminary notice, you should reference §8208 and §8210, make a formal request for identification of the lender and identification of the property owner, and, if any lenders are added after delivery of the preliminary notice, you should make a request for this as well. It is a good practice to make this request regardless of your confidence in the information you already have.

KEEP EVIDENCE OF SENDING AND DELIVERY

While we don't have the case law to support it, the terminology in the new preliminary notice section (Cal Civil Code §8200 et seq) seems clearer than the previous versions, and clear about one thing in particular: you must send your preliminary notices.

If you are looking to file a mechanics lien claim in the future, you'll need to prove that you properly delivered your preliminary notice. You must keep records not only of the parcel's delivery, but more importantly keep records proving that you sent the preliminary notice.

INCLUDE NEW STATUTORY LANGUAGE

Last, but certainly not least, make sure your preliminary notice form conforms to the law's new requirements. Aside from your form referencing the correct statute (§8200 et seq), one of the most obvious components of the form you'll need to have comply is the required text, which must be in **"boldface type:"**

By Scott G. Wolfe, Jr.   Published by Zlien

NOTICE TO PROPERTY OWNER EVEN THOUGH YOU HAVE PAID YOUR CONTRACTOR IN FULL, if the person or firm that has given you this notice is not paid in full for labor, service, equipment, or material provided or to be provided to your construction project, a lien may be placed on your property. Foreclosure of the lien may lead to loss of all or part of your property. You may wish to protect yourself against this by (1) requiring your contractor to provide a signed release by the person or firm that has given you this notice before making payment to your contractor, or (2) any other method that is appropriate under the circumstances. This notice is required by law to be served by the undersigned as a statement of your legal rights. This notice is not intended to reflect upon the financial condition of the contractor or the person employed by you on the construction project. If you record a notice of cessation or completion of your construction project, you must within 10 days after recording, send a copy of the notice of completion to your contractor and the person or firm that has given you this notice. The notice must be sent by registered or certified mail. Failure to send the notice will extend the deadline to record a claim of lien. You are not required to send the notice if you are a residential homeowner of a dwelling containing four or fewer units.

ARE THERE ANY EXCEPTIONS TO CALIFORNIA'S PRELIMINARY NOTICE REQUIREMENTS?

Short answer: Yes. There is a limited exception recognized by California Courts, but you should be very careful when relying upon it.

Long answer: As a general rule, if you did not contract directly with the property owner on a California construction project, you must deliver a "20 Day Preliminary Notice" within 20 days of first furnishing labor and/or materials to the construction project.

If you find yourself unpaid on a construction project when you failed to send a preliminary notice, there is one exception. However, it is a very limited exception, and you should be careful when relying on it because whether you are entitled to the exception or not will depend on a judge's decision. The decision could go either way because it's certain that the property owner will oppose your position, and the judge will be required to decide who is lying and who is telling the truth. Whenever a dispute comes down to this decision there is a large risk of loss.

Nevertheless, an exception has been recognized in <u>Truestone, Inc. v. SIMI West Industrial Park II</u>, 163 Cal.App. 3d 715 (Cal. App. 2d 1984). The courts held that an owner with actual knowledge of a particular party's involvement with a construction project cannot challenge a mechanic lien based on not having notice that the particular party was on the project.

Here are the court's words exactly:

In some cases, even where there is no contractual relationship between the parties, actual knowledge may stop the property owner from asserting the notice requirements of section 3097. The extent of the property owner's knowledge and the time it was acquired may be a significant variable. Section 3129 establishes a presumption that all construction work performed on property with the owner's knowledge "shall be held to have been constructed, performed, or furnished at the instance of such owner . . . ." Therefore, where a work of improvement is completed on leased land under contract with a lessee of the property, a statutory exception to the notice requirement of section 3097 applies.

"The noncontracting owner is placed in the position of a party to the contract by the conclusive presumption that the work was done at his instance and request." (Halspar, Inc. v. La Barthe (1965) 238 Cal.App.2d 897, 899 [48 Cal.Rptr. 293].) The lessor-owner with actual knowledge may be estopped to deny the validity of the lien because the lessee is viewed as his agent. (M. Arthur Gensler, Jr. & Associates, Inc. v. Larry Barrett, Inc. (1972) 7 Cal.3d 695, 707 [103 Cal.Rptr. 247, 499 P.2d 503].) Similarly, the lien of a firm which supplied architectural and engineering services to real property under a contract with the original owner-developer is enforceable against the subsequent transferees of the property on an estoppel theory. (Scott, Blake & Wynne v. Summit Ridge Estates, Inc. (1967) 251 Cal.App.2d 347 [59 Cal.Rptr. 587].)

Notice that the court says, "The extent of the property owner's knowledge and the time it was acquired may be a significant variable." This means the courts will have a very wide dissection in determining whether the knowledge was or was not sufficient to forgive a lien claimant for not sending its preliminary notice. It is a very thin exception to the preliminary notice rule but still an exception.

Therefore, if you did not send preliminary notice, you may have a chance at proceeding with your lien claim despite the defect in notice if the property owner knew you were on the project, knew you were performing work, and had that knowledge within 20 days of you first starting to furnish the labor and/or materials.

IS A 2ND NOTICE REQUIRED IF THE CONTRACT PRICE OR SCOPE CHANGES BY CHANGE ORDER?

Short Answer: No, the original California preliminary notice is effective for all work on the project, so long as the work is part of a single continuous contract.

Long Answer: A client recently contacted me about an on-going construction project that had already had a California preliminary notice sent on it. As anyone in the construction industry knows, orders changing the contract price and contract scope are commonplace. And as anyone who acts as a subcontractor or supplier in California knows, California preliminary notices require you describe the labor or materials being furnished and the estimated cost of said materials and labor.

If a change order is issued either increasing or decreasing the contract's scope or price what are the supplier or subcontractor's obligations with respect to California's preliminary notice requirements? Must a new California preliminary notice be sent to identify the modified scope or price?

This circumstance is directly addressed by the civil code provision addressing California preliminary notices, Cal. Civ. Code § 3097(g), providing:

A person required by this section to give notice to the owner, to an original

By Scott G. Wolfe, Jr.   Published by Zlien

contractor, and to a person to whom a notice to withhold may be given, need give only one notice...with respect to all materials, services, labor, or equipment he or she furnishes for a work of improvement, that means the entire structure or scheme of improvements as a whole, unless the same is furnished under contracts with more than one subcontractor, in which event, the notice requirements shall be met with respect to materials, services, labor, or equipment furnished to each contractor.

If a notice contains a general description required by subdivision (a) or (b) of the materials, services, labor, or equipment furnished to the date of notice, it is not defective because, after that date, the person giving notice furnishes materials, services, labor, or equipment not within the scope of this general description.

Subsection (c)(1) of this provision actually sets forth the requirement that each California preliminary notice contain a general description of the labor or materials to be furnished on the project, and an "estimate of the total price thereof." Since the statutes combine the "description" of the labor and materials with the estimate of its value, it would be considered one in the same.

Therefore, if either the scope of the work or the value of the work changes, § 3097(g)'s rule is going to apply, and you do not need to modify your California preliminary notice unless a separate contract with a separate party is executed.

YOUR NOTICE CAN NEVER BE SENT TOO EARLY

Preliminary notice statutes across the United States are written similar to California's statute, which requires all parties who did not contract with the property owner to deliver a preliminary notice within 20 days from first furnishing materials or labor to the project. This begs the question: Can preliminary notice be sent before you begin furnishing, or would that be a premature notice?

The answer is yes. The question has been answered in California in a number of cases, but the best explanation was published by the 4th District California Appeals Court in Brown Company v. Appellate Department, when the court explained as follows:

A preliminary notice to establish a claim of lien (CC § 3097) that was sent by a supplier of concrete before the concrete was delivered to the jobsite was not premature. The statute does not specify an initial date for serving the preliminary notice nor does it specify a date before which notice may not be given; it merely provides a deadline after which a preliminary notice may not be served. Moreover, the purpose of the preliminary notice requirement is to notify the owner, contractor, and lender of potential mechanic's lien claims. Allowing the notice to be given before work begins is consistent with the statutory purpose of giving notice, facilitates the constitutionally guaranteed right to claim for work or materials furnished, and avoids the absurd consequences that would result from a contrary interpretation. In addition, the word "claimant," as used in § 3097, was intended to include all potential lien claimants.

Material suppliers and subcontractors who contract for work months or even years before performing may wonder if they can send the preliminary notice at the time of contracting, or if they must wait until they begin furnishing materials or labor and then try to fit it within a small 20-day window. Based on prior California case law, you can send the notice at anytime, as there is no way to send your notice too early.

HOW TO FIND A LENDER ON A CALIFORNIA CONSTRUCTION PROJECT

To preserve the right to file a mechanics lien in California, subcontractors and suppliers are required to deliver a preliminary notice within 20 days of first furnishing work. That preliminary notice must be delivered to the property owner, the "director contractor" and the lender, if any. There has always been a dilemma with this requirement, however. Subcontractors and suppliers never had a way to know whether a lender existed, or who the lender was.

California's new mechanics lien law went into effect July 1st, 2012, and its §8208 and §8210 offers a solution to this long-standing problem in the state. These statutes provide:

§ 8208. A direct contractor shall make available to any person seeking to give preliminary notice the following information: (a) The name and address of the owner. (b) The name and address of the construction lender, if any.

§ 8210. If one or more construction loans are obtained after commencement of a work of improvement, the owner shall give notice of the name and address of the construction lender or lenders to each person that has given the owner preliminary notice.

THE GREAT NEWS – YOU CAN ASK FOR THE LENDER

The great news for subcontractors and suppliers is that direct contractors and property owners now have affirmative obligations to inform them of who is lending to the project. Prior to this amendment, it was common practice and courtesy for direct contractors to provide this type of preliminary notice information, but there wasn't a provision in the law requiring them to disclose this information.

Obviously, it is quite difficult for a lien claimant to unearth this information. It would require a trip to the recorders office and a scan of public records to see who last financed on the property. Multiply that expense times the number of projects most companies manage, and the expense was never quite worth the benefit. The law now makes clear that the information *shall* be made available to anyone required to deliver preliminary notice.

THE BAD NEWS – WHO KNOWS WHAT THIS MEANS?

You heard the great news, but let me dispense some bad news: the law is a little ambiguous and California attorneys cannot be sure what it means, how it will be interpreted, and what happens if the requirement is violated.

For example, §8208 requires only that a direct contractor "make available" the lending information. Does this mean it must be *distributed* to all subcontractors or suppliers, or may the direct contractor sit back and wait for the information to be directly requested?

By Scott G. Wolfe, Jr.   Published by Zlien

Once the information is requested, how long does the direct contractor have to reply with the information?

Additionally, what are the consequences when information is withheld, provided to the requesting party inaccurately, or if the direct contractor takes so long to get the information to the requestor that it defeats the purpose of sending the preliminary notice? I can see a court punishing a direct contractor or a property owner for failing to distribute the lending information, but will a court punish the innocent lender?

GENERAL CONTRACTORS MUST NOW SEND PRELIMINARY NOTICE

California's mechanics lien law changed significantly on July 1st, 2012. One change to the preliminary notice provisions affects those who contract directly with the property owner. These previously exempt parties **must** now deliver a preliminary notice.

§8200(e)(2) of California's new preliminary notice laws states that those "with a direct contractual relationship with an owner or reputed owner is required to give preliminary notice only to the construction lender or reputed construction lender, if any."

This is a significant change to the mechanics lien laws that will probably go unnoticed by "direct contractors," which are a category of constructors that includes many participants from handymen to huge general contracting outfits. For years, direct contracts were not required to deliver a preliminary notice to preserve their mechanics lien rights. Current law in California, however, makes the reverse true.

DIRECT CONTRACTORS IN CALIFORNIA MUST DELIVER PRELIMINARY NOTICE TO THE LENDER

As per the quote of California Civil Code §8200, direct contractors must now furnish preliminary notice to the construction lender. This requirement only applies if there is a construction lender on the project. If there is a lender, the lender must receive the notice.

By Scott G. Wolfe, Jr.   Published by Zlien

If there is not a lender, the direct contractor doesn't have a notice requirement.

What is a "construction lender?"

> § 8006. *"Construction lender" means either of the following: (a) A mortgagee or beneficiary under a deed of trust lending funds with which the cost of all or part of a work of improvement is to be paid, or the assignee or successor in interest of the mortgagee or beneficiary. (b) An escrow holder or other person holding funds provided by an owner, lender, or another person as a fund for with which the cost of all or part of a work of improvement is to be paid.*

The key point to remember is that a regular mortgage on the property is not a "construction lender," and direct contractors (or any other project participants) are required to give notice to standard mortgages on the property. A lender only qualifies as a "construction lender" if they contributed funds to the work of improvement itself.

For example, if a homeowner remodels their kitchen, and they pay for it with their own savings, they will not have a "construction lender" even though the home may have a mortgage. However, if that same homeowner took out a loan for the remodel, or incorporated the remodel into some refinancing agreement with the original mortgage, then a construction lender does likely exist and preliminary notice is required.

HOW TO PREPARE AND DELIVER THE CALIFORNIA PRELIMINARY NOTICE

If you are a direct contractor, you may never have delivered a California preliminary notice in the past. It is a rather simple process, and you can even outsource the work. First you need to fill out the California form in as much detail as possible. If you don't know who the lender is, you are entitled to get that information from the property owner.

Second, you need to send the notice for delivery. You should send the notice by certified mail. Since you must later prove that notice was sent and delivered, it is a good idea to draft an Affidavit of Mailing or Affidavit of Service making note of exactly when, how, and who sent the parcel. Keep track of the mailing, make sure it is delivered, and then record evidence of that delivery from the USPS.

RESEARCH VERY IMPORTANT WHEN SENDING PRELIMINARY NOTICES

When sending preliminary notices, it is important to have the right form and to follow all statutory requirements in your sending method. An often-overlooked aspect of preparing a preliminary notice is doing project research to make sure you're sending the notice to the right people. This research and data verification is critical. Sending notice to the wrong person is a common error.

WHAT YOU NEED TO VERIFY WITH EVERY PRELIMINARY NOTICE

When doing data research and verification about a construction project you are focused on two key concerns: (i) whether you are sending the correct form, and (ii) whether you are sending your form to the right parties.

WHY DATA RESEARCH MATTERS TO WHICH FORM YOU ARE SENDING

Finding a preliminary notice form may seem easy enough, but there are some hidden complications. Preliminary notice forms will obviously change from state-to-state, but they also change depending on the type of project, your role in the project, and your tier. The most striking form differences occur between private, state and federal projects. These different project types are governed by completely different sets of laws with very, very little overlap.

Residential projects sometimes have different forms from commercial projects, and even owner-occupied residential projects require different treatment from ordinary residential projects. In the state context, highway projects are sometimes treated differently from other state public works.

Data research is crucial to determine exactly what type of project you're working on, and enable you to choose and send the correct preliminary notice form. Determining if a project is residential or commercial, or state or private can be very ambiguous.

By Scott G. Wolfe, Jr.   Published by Zlien

Here are some common challenges:

- Apartment and condominium complexes pose a challenge because they can sometimes be considered commercial and at other times residential depending on the scope of work

- Many states are engaging in public-private partnerships to build certain centers, and this creates confusion as to whether the project is public or private

- Private companies sometimes lease space from public entities and perform improvements thereon

- Schools and universities can be public or private depending on their organization

WHY DATA RESEARCH MATTERS FOR WHO RECEIVES YOUR FORM

Figuring out the project type can be the easy part. Once you have your project type and preliminary notice form settled, the next consideration is who exactly should receive the form. This does not refer to which project participants in the big picture sense are statutorily required to receive the form, but about which specific people and companies are required to receive the form.

Identifying the form recipient is a challenge for construction companies because it requires them to determine the identity of parties like the property owner, general contractor, and construction lender, when they might not otherwise know who these parties are. Frequently, even when these parties are identified to the claimant, the identification was incorrect.

Here are some common issues:

- A party is identified to you as a property owner, but they are actually a tenant who commissioned the work. The notice will usually still go to the property owner and you must do property owner research.

- You must notify the construction lender in states like California, Arizona and Oregon, but the lender isn't frequently identified to you. You are required, therefore, to research the construction lender's identity.

By Scott G. Wolfe, Jr.   Published by Zlien

- A property owner is identified to you as a person, when it is actually the person's company that owns the property.

- The property owner is identified to you as a single person, but they are actually married and jointly own the property.

There are more than a thousand mistakes that can be made when identifying the property owner, the tenant, the general contractor and other parties to a construction project. Doing research on the front end is important, and it is something that should be done with every single preliminary notice sent.

ZLIEN HELPS YOU RESEARCH PRELIMINARY NOTICE DATA

Outsourcing the research of preliminary notice data is important, and is the reason I started Zlien seven years ago. Instead of relying on an employee who only prepares and sends these notices periodically, you will have a professional set of eyes taking a look at your data and checking it against available public records databases. This is particularly important given the room for error in identifying necessary parties, adhering to detailed state-by-state regulations, and maintaining proof of delivery. It could mean the difference between enforceable lien rights, and no lien rights at all.

Note that it is the preliminary notice service and outsourcing that makes the difference here, and that is why I've always advocated a service over software. Preliminary notice software is a good start for your company, but it is not a real solution. It leaves you vulnerable to mistakes in data research and verification, and it also costs your company unnecessary time and expense.

1 THING ALMOST EVERYONE FORGETS WHEN SENDING PRELIMINARY NOTICES

Hundreds of thousands of preliminary notices are sent in California in-house by companies every year, and they nearly always forget a very crucial requirement: Filling out and signing a declaration of delivery.

By Scott G. Wolfe, Jr.   Published by Zlien

WHEN A DECLARATION IS REQUIRED UNDER CALIFORNIA'S PRELIMINARY NOTICE LAWS

A declaration is always required. California Civil Code §8118 requires it as a component of every single California preliminary notice when it provides that "Proof that notice was given to a person in the manner required by this part shall be made by a proof of notice declaration that states all of the following..." There are many curiosities in this statute, and a savvy litigator could really put some pressure on a lien claimant based on this statue and how frequently it is overlooked.

First, based on the language, it is a bit ambiguous as to whether the declaration must be made upon sending every single notice, or if it is only required if a party must to "prove" that it was sent. There are many occasions when such proof may not be required. For example, a party may admit receipt of the preliminary notice. A lawyer could argue that based on §8118, the preliminary notice was not properly sent unless a declaration was prepared and signed upon delivery.

Second, in the instance when a party does deny receiving the notice, it would be curious if a court would allow the claimant to retroactively prepare one of these declarations. Could they, in other words, have the person who mailed the notice fill out the declaration after-the-fact (perhaps months later) if proof was required to demonstrate compliance with the preliminary notice requirement? One point is for sure under the California statute - having postal records of delivery is not enough to prove notice was sent. You must have the declaration as well.

WHAT IS A DECLARATION OF SERVICE?

This leads to the inevitable question: What exactly is a declaration of service? A California declaration of service or delivery is a very simple document. It is a signed statement by the person who performed the service (i.e. the person who mailed the notice) identifying themselves, identifying when the notice was sent, identifying that it was a preliminary notice sent, and identifying who it was sent to and how. A free Declaration of Service of Preliminary Notice is made available for you to download on the Zlien website.

By Scott G. Wolfe, Jr.   Published by Zlien

IT'S SMART TO OUTSOURCE PRELIMINARY NOTICE WORK

It is worth reiterating that outsourcing your preliminary notice work is a good idea legally and financially. It is not impossible to send preliminary notices yourself. It is not impossible to find software – quite good software – to prepare notice forms for you so you can have your staff prepare the notices and send them. Doing it yourself comes at both a high risk of error and an unnecessarily high expense. The requirements pile onto one another and it becomes very difficult to comply with the notice requirements on every project. Hiring a company like Zlien to manage and send your preliminary notices is a smart decision.

EVEN LATE PRELIMINARY NOTICES ARE WORTH SENDING

Whenever a state requires preliminary notices, those notices must be sent within a certain time frame. Normally, the period for sending notice is calculated from the first day your company furnishes labor or materials to the project. However, some states require notice within just 8 days (Oregon) and others allow as long as 60 days (Washington).

The general rule is that if you are required to send preliminary notice, and you don't send it, you have no lien rights whatsoever. There is a tiny, tiny exception to this rule that may apply to your project, and that is the concept of sending late preliminary notices.

In most states that require preliminary notices, if a notice is sent late, it is effective as to materials or labor furnished just before the notice is sent. The "bubble of effectiveness" stretches backwards for the period of time that the preliminary notice is required.

For example, if you are in Washington, preliminary notice is required within 60 days of first furnishing labor or materials. If you send this preliminary notice late, it will still be effective to preserve your lien rights for any labor or material furnished after you send the notice, and for 60 days before the notice is sent.

Likewise, in California, notice is required within 20 days of first furnishing labor or material.

By Scott G. Wolfe, Jr.   Published by Zlien

A late preliminary notice will be effective for all labor or material furnished after the notice is sent, and for 20 days before the notice is sent.

The earlier you send the notice the better, especially for companies like material suppliers who frequently only send shipments once or twice. However, if you are constantly working on a project and forget to send your notice, it may be worth it to send the preliminary notice late.

By Scott G. Wolfe, Jr.   Published by Zlien

CHAPTER 4

Why Notice Is Important And How To Do It Right?

PRELIMINARY NOTICES WILL NOT SCARE YOUR CUSTOMER

Not wanting to send a preliminary notice from fear you will "ruin a relationship" or "put a client on alert," is a common misconception. There are many reasons why notices are always a good business practice.

PROPERTY OWNERS AND PRIME CONTRACTORS EXPECT IT AND GET TONS

On construction projects in states where preliminary notices are required, property owners and prime contractors will receive many pre-lien notices, and they *expect* to receive them.

On any given project, there may be fifty or one hundred different trades, suppliers, equipment rental companies and consultants. Some of these companies are small, but many of them are medium or large outfits that furnish materials or labor to projects across the country. Of all these companies, those with quality credit policies are disciplined and send preliminary notices on every single project.

A property owner or prime contractor to an ordinary ground-up project or major renovation will likely receive more than twenty or thirty notices. No one gets terminated because of them. Instead, they get filed away, and in most cases, the property owner and prime contractor *appreciate* that you sent the notice because it alerts them that you value your work, and gives a good first impression that your company is organized.

By Scott G. Wolfe, Jr.   Published by Zlien

IT'S NOT ADVERSARIAL AND HARD TO MISTAKE FOR A LIEN

A preliminary notice is not an adversarial document. It makes no demand for payment, and it is very hard to mistake for a lien. In fact, it very commonly states at the top of the notice in all-caps bold face type: "THIS IS NOT A LIEN."

In all my years of practicing construction law and helping companies send preliminary notices through Zlien, I've never had a preliminary notice mistaken for a lien, or heard a single complaint from someone who has received a preliminary notice. None of my clients have ever lost a customer because they sent off preliminary notices.

Additionally, put aside for a second the misconception that you have a *choice* in sending your preliminary notice. In many states, the law makes it *mandatory* that you send these notices. If you do not send the notices, you are technically subject to penalty by a state regulatory body. Louisiana and Washington are examples of this regulation.

IT CAN BE SENT "NICELY"

Finally, the notice can be sent "nicely." When we send preliminary notices through Zlien, for example, these notices go out in an unbranded envelope that says "Zlien Preliminary Notices Division." In addition, many of our notices state something along these lines in its opening to put the receiving party at ease: "Hello! This preliminary notice is sent according to our policy to keep our customers and their customers informed about who is working on their construction projects…."

GET FINED IF YOU DON'T SEND PRELIMINARY NOTICE

California's new mechanics lien laws are serious about their preliminary notice requirements. Under the new statutes, failing to send a preliminary notice will not only forfeit your mechanics lien, bond claim or stop payment notice rights, but it will also earn you a fine from the California Contractors' State Licensing Board. This fine is not unheard of in the world of mechanics lien laws.

By Scott G. Wolfe, Jr.   Published by Zlien

California Civil Code §8216 provides for the penalty:

"If the contract of any subcontractor on a particular work of improvement provides for payment to the subcontractor of more than four hundred dollars ($400), the failure of that subcontractor…to give the [preliminary] notice provided for in this chapter, constitutes grounds for disciplinary action under the Contractors' State License Law."

It is important to remember that this statute only applies to subcontractors and only in those instances when the subcontract amount is over $400, but these are quite meager limitations and this provision will apply in a vast majority of cases for subcontractors.

When consulting with companies about creating a mechanics lien policy and sending preliminary notices to preserve lien rights on every project, one of the frequent hesitations is that the party doesn't want to send preliminary notices because they have "relationships" to preserve at the project, and they don't want to scare off their customers or business.

There are hundreds of reasons why this fear is misplaced. California Civil Code §8216 threatening "disciplinary action" upon subcontractors is a reminder that preliminary notices are a fact of business in the construction world. Property owners and prime contractors get tons of them on every project and will not be offended by yours. Most importantly, it is mandated by law that you do send them, or face discipline.

4 REASONS YOU'RE WRONG IF YOU THINK PRELIMINARY NOTICES ARE BAD BUSINESS

When talking to clients about preserving their mechanics lien rights by setting up a lien policy that sends preliminary notices on each project, Zlien frequently gets pushed back with worries that preliminary notices will scare others on the project or impair relationships.

By Scott G. Wolfe, Jr.   Published by Zlien

1. Preliminary Notices Are A Fact of Life In Construction And You're Probably In The Minority If You Don't Send Them

In states where preliminary notice is required, everyone is sending them. Most general contractors even have software to manage the preliminary notices they receive since there are so many.

As an attorney, I've represented a lot of general contractors and developers. I have *never ever* seen any push back or concern from these parties because they received a preliminary notice. It is a complete non-issue. The extremely rare occasion when someone does get rattled by these notices is because they are inexperienced and unsophisticated. These are exactly the parties you want to be cautious about, which makes the preliminary notice even more important.

2. Your Fear of Preliminary Notices Is Unfounded, As You Take Other Credit Protection Measures Without As Much Fear

It seems that credit managers and construction controllers are more fearful of preliminary notices than they are about *much more* invasive measures like joint check agreements and letters of credit. There is no good reason. Credit is credit and protection is protection. Mechanics lien rights – preserved through preliminary notices – are the least invasive credit protection you can get, and the most effective.

3. Preliminary Notices Are Sometimes Required By Law, Giving You No Choice

If you think sending a preliminary notice is optional, you may be wrong depending on where you are furnishing. Since July 1, 2012, the State of California has made preliminary notices mandatory, and companies can actually get fined for not sending the notice. Cases like this have already occurred in other states. .

4. Preliminary Notices Are Not Liens, Do Not Threaten Liens and Are Not Scary

A lot of companies (and sales departments) fear preliminary notices simply because they do not understand them. They think they are liens, or that they threaten liens, or that they are an abrasive document that will make demands and threats to their customers. However, preliminary notices are nothing like this. They are simply notices that are required by law, and that inform the receiving party that the law protects all materialmen and subcontractors from non-payment with the lien remedy. In fact, notices are designed by state courts to help the owner and the general contractor protect themselves against bad situations.

SEND PRELIMINARY NOTICES EVERY TIME BECAUSE YOUR BEST CLIENTS CAN FAIL TOO

"We only want to send preliminary notice on our riskier accounts," is a statement that can put your company in quick financial trouble.

YOUR BEST CLIENTS ARE YOUR BIGGEST RISK!

Companies make credit decisions everyday, extending more credit to those companies who are more credit-worthy. The art of extending credit is an art, and not a science. Every time you extend credit to a company you make a series of judgments. Sometimes, a company can accumulate good credit with your company (and bigger lines) for just being a good customer, and without much regard for the company's actual financial affairs outside of its involvement with you.

Making these credit decisions is tough because companies in financial trouble never advertise their impending doom. Your bigger clients are the bigger risk because you have the most to lose with their accounts, and their accounts are no more foolproof than your smaller clients. This concept is illustrated in the following case study:

A client furnishes materials nationwide and one of their better customers had over $750,000 of materials in-hand when the customer was put into receivership. The customer's liabilities so outnumbered their assets that the client had slim chances of seeing any of that money in the receivership action. This was a really great customer with a large credit line, but what now?

Fortunately, the client's practice was to send preliminary notices on every project, which

---

By Scott G. Wolfe, Jr.   Published by Zlien

meant that its lien and bond claim rights were protected on this customer's account. It filed a collection of 7-10 mechanics liens and bond claims and collected virtually every penny owed to it without having to spend legal efforts and money in the receivership.

NEVERTHELESS, SOME PRELIMINARY NOTICES ARE BETTER THAN NONE

In a perfect world you would send preliminary notices on every project, but there are reasons why some clients choose otherwise. There are quality reasons for these decisions. It's just another credit decision for a company.

I've written about these decisions in the past when I wrote articles about Lien Policies, and Creating a Lien Policy. When companies are implementing a preliminary notice and mechanics lien program they must draw lines designating who will get notices and who will not, when liens will be filed and when they will not. Programs can be aggressive or conservative. One size does not fit all.

Nevertheless, preliminary notices and mechanics liens should be at least some part of every company's credit policy and credit management programs.

PRELIMINARY NOTICE SOFTWARE...OR A SERVICE?

When it comes to sending preliminary notices, outsourcing the work is the smart choice for your company.

EVERY SECOND AND DIME YOU SPEND ON SOFTWARE IS A WASTE

You are in the construction business, not the computer and software business. Software must be updated, it costs money, it takes infrastructure and tech support, it requires training, it crashes, it contains so many features that it's hard to keep tract, it is built for a general need and not your specific need, and the list goes on and on.

A competitor offering preliminary notice service (Tradition Software) published an update on its blog that illustrates the waste of software:

By Scott G. Wolfe, Jr.   Published by Zlien

PreLien2Lien v. 16.07.01 will be available for download from this website on Friday, June 29th. This new version will do a find/replace to update the CALIFORNIA notices for the software. TRADITION SOFTWARE's Customer Service Department will be calling customers who have custom templates for CALIFORNIA to help install any templates that need changes for the new laws. [Misspelling in the original]

No one wants to take the time, energy and expertise to continually update all of their computers with this software. No one wants to take the risk that they don't have the latest software where there is a new case update in countless states. Additionally, software can cost up to $700 per user with annual subscription fees up to $300. Altogether, software is a waste of both time and money.

SOFTWARE LEAVES YOU TO DO EVERYTHING – AND THERE IS A LOT TO DO

There is a long list of tasks your staff <u>must do</u> when sending every single notice:

5. Determine if the project is a state, federal, commercial or residential project

6. Find the property owner (the actual one)

7. Find the lender

8. Fill out the form or input the data into software

9. Print the forms, envelopes, envelope labels

10. Apply postage to your envelopes, and prepare certified mail slips

11. Prepare a declaration of delivery and sign it

12. Save everything someplace

13. Track the mailings, and if any come back, re-mail it by doing #s 4-8 again

Forgetting or doing any one of these things wrong could be fatal to your mechanics lien rights.

By Scott G. Wolfe, Jr.   Published by Zlien

OUTSOURCING YOUR NOTICES IS CHEAPER THAN SENDING THEM YOURSELF

I know it <u>feels</u> like you are saving money by sending preliminary notices in-house, but you are absolutely not. Let's look at the true costs of sending preliminary notices yourself:

THE COSTS IN MONEY

First consider the real nuts and bolts spending. Since California is a large state and has a common preliminary notice framework, we can consider this state for cost estimating.

- Postage for 3 Mailings, Certified Mail (owner, lender, prime): $18

- Envelopes, Labels, Paper, Ink: $0.70

- Labor Paid To Your Employee, based on 15 minutes per project and a $45,000/yr salary: $5.63

- The software cost as determined by dividing the number of projects you send notices out on each year by the cost paid for the software and support each year (Example of 240 projects per year and $1000 per year: $4.17)

Total Cost: $27.87 per project.

For comparison, Zlien sends and manages your preliminary notices for $27 per project. Depending on your volume, it can be as little as $21 per project.

THE NEGATIVE COSTS TO YOUR COMPANY

The cost in money is high, but the costs in time and productivity for your staff can be higher. The employees completing and sending these forms, and researching each project's property owner and lender, could be doing better things with their time. Making you money. Talking with clients, checking on projects, responding to emails that could get a punch list item done before the end of the today instead of tomorrow. How much money are you losing by taking that precious time and spending it on sending your own preliminary notices, at the above build-in expenses?

YOU'RE GOING TO MESS UP. REALLY.

If you have sent preliminary notices on your own for years and never ran into a problem, you are giving yourself into a false sense of security. I can guarantee you have made fatal mistakes on your preliminary notices at some point, but just do not realize it because you got lucky, and the project was paid.

Companies sending their own preliminary notices make mistakes all the time. It is expected and understandable. It is not your job. It is not your top priority. When you use a service to send your preliminary notices, you are getting a company completely focused on making sure your notices are right, every time.

---

4 REASONS IT'S SMART TO OUTSOURCE YOUR PRELIMINARY NOTICE WORK

Filing a mechanic's lien can be the difference between collecting your debt, or not. If you are doing work or supplying equipment or materials on a project that requires delivery of a preliminary notice, you will be left without lien rights unless you deliver that preliminary notice pretty immediately after first furnishing any labor or materials. Not only must the preliminary notice be timely, it must also be correct. Preparing and delivering your own notices could be a recipe for disaster. Here are four reasons why it is smart for your company to outsource its preliminary notice work.

PRELIMINARY NOTICES ARE TECHNICAL, WITH LOTS OF ROOM FOR ERROR

There is no single "preliminary notice" form that can be used in any state and any situation. What your notice must say *can and will* differ depending on where you're working (i.e. state), what type of project you're working on (i.e. private, state, federal) and in what tier you fall.

State statutes can get very particular about the notice's wording, oftentimes requiring the notices to contain specific language in a certain font-size, bold and/or in all caps.

By Scott G. Wolfe, Jr.   Published by Zlien

Statutes are also picky about how notices must be sent, who they must be sent to, and how you will need to prove that you actually sent the notice.

Take the state of California, for example. There is a 20-day preliminary notice required on private construction projects in California that must contain a statement identical to the one required in California Civil Code §3084 in "10-point boldface type." Plus, §3084(a)(6) also requires that the sending party maintain a "proof of service affidavit" and any records of mailing (i.e. the certified mail record).

If you wanted to send this notice yourself, you would have to make sure you had the right form. The California law changed January 1, 2011, so be careful which sites you trust. Then, you would have to make sure you send it to the right people (the owner, the prime and the lender), that you send it in the right way, and that you maintain the correct proof of delivery (affidavit and mail record). There is, as you can see, a lot of opportunity for error.

Outsourcing your preliminary notice work makes this entire process very simple. Here at Zlien, for example, you simply give us the project details, and we make sure the appropriate form gets to the appropriate places in the appropriate way. Everything you need to prove it was sent will be permanently saved for you on our online servers.

TIME SPENT WORKING ON PRELIMINARY NOTICES IS TIME WASTED FOR YOUR COMPANY

Your employees already have a lot to do, and the things they do make your company money. Whether they are doing project management work, or accounting work, it is unlikely that you have an employee 100% dedicated to sending preliminary notices.

Most of the time, if a company sends its preliminary notices at all, they will pick someone on their staff to prepare and send these notices. Whenever a notice is required, this employee has to interrupt his or her workday to figure out which notice to send, how to send it, and then to put together the notice and mailing. If the employee does it 100% correct, they will spend at least 15-25 minutes for each notice.

Is it worth that amount of time? Is it worth taking that employee away from things that

By Scott G. Wolfe, Jr.   Published by Zlien

make your company money for them to work on these technical and time consuming preliminary notices? The answer is most certainly "no," especially in light of how much outsourcing can save you in real money.

PROFESSIONAL QUALITY CONTROL

When you outsource your preliminary notice work, the company preparing your notices will likely not only be preparing and sending the form as required by applicable statutes, but they will also be checking the project data.

At Zlien, we very frequently find errors with the identified property owner or property address. Frequently, an address won't have the direction (N, E, S, W) properly listed, or a property owner will just be incorrect (i.e. reference to individual rather than a business entity).

Instead of relying on an employee who only prepares and sends these notices periodically, you will have a professional set of eyes looking at your data and checking it against available public records databases. It could mean the difference between enforceable lien rights, and no lien rights at all.

FINALLY, IT MAKES FINANCIAL SENSE

Looking at how much it actually costs you to send your own preliminary notices, the conclusion is clear.

First, you have the employee, whose time is not free. Take an employee who gets paid $50,000 per year. On average, a full-time employee works 2,000 hours, making a $50k per year employee compensated at a rate of $25.00 per hour. A California 20-day preliminary notice must be sent to three parties, and will take between 45 minutes and 1 hr 15 minutes to properly send. That will cost between $18.75 and $31.25 per project.

Second, you need to pay for postage. A certified mail return receipt request is typically $5.85, which times three, equals $17.55.

By Scott G. Wolfe, Jr.   Published by Zlien

Third, you can't forget your paper and envelopes. On average, this is $0.16 per notice, which is $0.48 for three notices.

Considering only these three cost elements (there are more), you are going to spend between $36.78 and $49.28 per project to send preliminary notices. If you outsource all of your notice work to Zlien, the most *expensive* plan offered charges you $28.00 per project to send all of your preliminary notices.

By Scott G. Wolfe, Jr.   Published by Zlien

California Preliminary Notice For Private Projects Form & Instructions

1. This notice form should be used for private construction projects only, which include residential, commercial and industrial projects, but exclude government, state, county or federal projects.

2. Service this notice on the following parties: (i) The owner or reputed owner; (ii) The direct contractor; and (iii) The construction lender, if any.

3. Serve the preliminary notice by either (i) hand delivery; or (ii) First class registered or certified mail, maining a proof of delivery and affidavit of delivery.

4. Complete the affidavit of delivery.

By Scott G. Wolfe, Jr.   Published by Zlien

PRELIMINARY NOTICE

IN ACCORDANCE WITH SECTIONS 8200 ET SEQ. AND 9300 ET SEQ., CALIFORNIA CIVIL CODE, THIS IS NOT A REFLECTION OF THE INTEGRITY OF ANY CONTRACTOR OR SUBCONTRACTOR.

NOTICE TO:

Property Owner:

Name & Address

YOU ARE HEREBY NOTIFIED THAT the Claimant has furnished or will be furnishing labor, services, equipment or materials of the following general description:

Direct Contractor:

Name & Address

These services have been contracted for by the Hiring Party (Name & Address):

Construction Lender:

Name & Address

An estimate of the total price of the labor, services, equipment or material furnished or to be furnished is:
$_____

NOTICE FROM:

Claimant:

Name & Address

Property Address where labor, services, equipment or materials are furnished or to be furnished:

IMPORTANT NOTICE ON FOLLOWING PAGE

By Scott G. Wolfe, Jr.   Published by Zlien

NOTICE TO PROPERTY OWNER

EVEN THOUGH YOU HAVE PAID YOUR CONTRACTOR IN FULL, if the person or firm that has given you this notice is not paid in full for labor, service, equipment, or material provided or to be provided to your construction project, a lien may lead to loss of all or part of your property. You may wish to protect yourself against this by (1) requiring your contractor to provide a signed release by the person or firm that has given you this notice before making payment to your contractor, or (2) any other method that is appropriate under the circumstances.

This notice is required by law to be served by the undersigned as a statement of your legal rights. This notice is not intended to reflect upon the financial condition of the contractor or the person employed by you on the construction project.

If you record a notice of cessation or completion of your construction project, you must within 10 days after recording, send a copy of the notice of completion to your contractor and the person or firm that has given you this notice. The notice must be sent by registered or certified mail. Failure to send the notice will extend the deadline to record a claim of lien. You are not required to send the notice if you are a residential homeowner of a dwelling containing four or fewer units.

IMPORTANT: INFORMATION REQUEST PURSUANT TO §8208

If the property owner and/or construction lender are not identified in this notice, or if either are incorrectly identified, please accept this notice as a formal request to the direct contractor pursuant to §8208 to deliver (i) The name and address of the owner; and /or (ii) The name and address of the construction lender, if any; as the case may be, to the Claimant at the above-provided address.

_____ (Signature)

Claimant

Signed by _____ (Name)

It's _____ (Title)

Dated: ___ /___ /_____

By Scott G. Wolfe, Jr.   Published by Zlien

PROOF OF SERVICE AFFIDAVIT

I, _____, declare that on the ____ day of _____, 20_____, I served copies of the attached Preliminary Notice to the following parties (If sent by certified or registered mail, with the included tracking numbers from the United States Postal Service):

[___] By personally delivering the notice to the above identified;

[___] By First Class Certified or Registered Mail service, postage prepaid, and addressed to the party at the address shown above.

I declare under penalty of perjury that the foregoing is true and correct. Signed in _____ County of the State of _____, on the _____ day of _____, 20_____.

_____ (Signature)

Claimant

Signed by _____ (Name)

It's _____ (Title)

Dated: ___ / ___ / _____

By Scott G. Wolfe, Jr.   Published by Zlien

California Preliminary Notice For State, County, Municipal Projects Form & Instructions

1. This notice form should be used for state construction projects only, which include municipal, county, city and state projects, but exclude privately owned commercial, residential or industrial projects.

2. Service this notice on the following parties: (i) The public entity commissioning work; (ii) The direct contractor; and (iii) The surety.

3. Serve the preliminary notice by either (i) hand delivery; or (ii) First class registered or certified mail, maining a proof of delivery and affidavit of delivery.

4. Complete the affidavit of delivery.

By Scott G. Wolfe, Jr.   Published by Zlien

PRELIMINARY NOTICE

IN ACCORDANCE WITH SECTIONS 8200 ET SEQ. AND 9300 ET SEQ., CALIFORNIA CIVIL CODE, THIS IS NOT A REFLECTION OF THE INTEGRITY OF ANY CONTRACTOR OR SUBCONTRACTOR.

NOTICE TO:

Public Entity:

Name & Address

YOU ARE HEREBY NOTIFIED THAT the Claimant has furnished or will be furnishing labor, services, equipment or materials of the following general description:

Direct Contractor:

Name & Address

These services have been contracted for by the Hiring Party (Name & Address):

Surety:

Name & Address

An estimate of the total price of the labor, services, equipment or material furnished or to be furnished is:
$_____

NOTICE FROM:

Claimant:

Name & Address

Identification of Project where labor, services, equipment or materials are furnished or to be furnished:

IMPORTANT NOTICE ON FOLLOWING PAGE

By Scott G. Wolfe, Jr.   Published by Zlien

NOTICE TO PROPERTY OWNER

EVEN THOUGH YOU HAVE PAID YOUR CONTRACTOR IN FULL, if the person or firm that has given you this notice is not paid in full for labor, service, equipment, or material provided or to be provided to your construction project, a lien may lead to loss of all or part of your property. You may wish to protect yourself against this by (1) requiring your contractor to provide a signed release by the person or firm that has given you this notice before making payment to your contractor, or (2) any other method that is appropriate under the circumstances.

This notice is required by law to be served by the undersigned as a statement of your legal rights. This notice is not intended to reflect upon the financial condition of the contractor or the person employed by you on the construction project.

If you record a notice of cessation or completion of your construction project, you must within 10 days after recording, send a copy of the notice of completion to your contractor and the person or firm that has given you this notice. The notice must be sent by registered or certified mail. Failure to send the notice will extend the deadline to record a claim of lien. You are not required to send the notice if you are a residential homeowner of a dwelling containing four or fewer units.

IMPORTANT: INFORMATION REQUEST PURSUANT TO §8208

If the public entity and/or surety are not identified in this notice, or if either are incorrectly identified, please accept this notice as a formal request to the direct contractor pursuant to §8208 to deliver (i) The name and address of the public entity; and /or (ii) The name and address of the surety, if any; as the case may be, to the Claimant at the above-provided address.

_____ (Signature)

Claimant

Signed by _____ (Name)

It's _____ (Title)

Dated: ___ /___ /_____

By Scott G. Wolfe, Jr.   Published by Zlien

PROOF OF SERVICE AFFIDAVIT

I, _____, declare that on the _____ day of _____, 20_____, I served copies of the attached Preliminary Notice to the following parties (If sent by certified or registered mail, with the included tracking numbers from the United States Postal Service):

[___] By personally delivering the notice to the above identified;

[___] By First Class Certified or Registered Mail service, postage prepaid, and addressed to the party at the address shown above.

I declare under penalty of perjury that the foregoing is true and correct. Signed in _____ County of the State of _____, on the _____ day of _____, 20_____.

_____ (Signature)

Claimant

Signed by _____ (Name)

It's _____ (Title)

Dated: ___ / ___ / _____

By Scott G. Wolfe, Jr.   Published by Zlien

www.ingramcontent.com/pod-product-compliance
Lightning Source LLC
Chambersburg PA
CBHW081242180526
45171CB00005B/516